EN ROUTE TO A MILLION

The Hardest Part Isn't Making The Money, It's Maintaining It.

S.M. Mahoney

Created by Money Luxury
MoneyLuxuryLtd@gmail.com
Twitter: @MoneyLuxuries
Instagram: MoneyLuxuries
Facebook: Money Luxury
www.MoneyLuxury.co.uk

Money Luxury
Self-Published by S.M Mahoney
Edited by the Paper True Team

Visit us on the World Wide Web:
http://www.MoneyLuxury.co.uk

Copyright © 2016 by S.M. Mahoney
All rights reserved, including the right of reproduction.
In whole or in part in any form.

ISBN: 978-0-9935801-0-9

Disclaimer

(PLEASE READ CAREFULLY)

Any information or opinions provided in *En Route To A Million* created by Money Luxury is general information; it does not take into account your personal circumstances. So please do not invest or trade based solely on this information. By viewing any material provided by Money Luxury, our website, resources or using the information we provide, you agree that this is general educational material and you will not hold any person or entity responsible for any loss or damages resulting from the content or general advice provided here by Money Luxury, its employees, directors or fellow members.

Leveraged forex markets, CFDs, futures, options and spot currency trading have large potential rewards, but also large potential risks. You must be aware of the risks and be willing to accept them in order to invest. Always trade with money you can afford to lose and remember that past results are not necessarily going to repeat in the future. No representation is being made that any account will or is likely to achieve profits or losses similar to those discussed in any material provided by Money Luxury.

Consumers of Money Luxury and readers of our books are responsible for their own investments, trading accounts and their own trades. Money Luxury is not responsible for any financial loss suffered by any student or reader from leveraged trading or any other financial investment. Money Luxury does not give investment advice and any opinions expressed or discussions that take place in this book cannot be deemed to be investment advice. Your financial trading account, trades carried out on your account and funds held in your account are a matter between you and your financial trading account provider. Any issues in these areas are to be settled between you and your trading platform provider and are not the responsibility of Money Luxury. The past performance of any trading system or methodology is not necessarily indicative of future results.

Nothing in this guidebook is intended to be a recommendation to buy or sell any financial instrument, futures or options market. Even if it may sound like we are urging you to do something, it is just figuratively speaking. A good amount of information is general and has been obtained from sources over a long period, which is believed to be reliable, but accuracy and thoroughness cannot be guaranteed. Readers are solely responsible for how they use the information and for their results.

For general enquiries, additional information concerning our legal policies or compliance issues regarding your account please send an e-mail to moneyluxuryltd@gmail.com.

Acknowledgements

A big thank you to everyone at Money Luxury and to everyone who has contributed and supported the creation of our first book. It has been a long but worthwhile process, which was made easier with the help of the people who gave a helping hand or their expertise. Thanks to all of our editors and contributors; the editors at Paper True, Emma Lawrence, Richard Miller, Jared Martinez, Francis Fabrizi, Ore Bammeke, Jason Perempillah and a bigger thank you to my parents for all their support along this journey. Also want to give credit to Shutterstock and Freepik for the images used in this book.

It takes a lot of thought, time and effort to complete a book, which contains many different factors, different sections and many different roles needed for a variety of tasks to reach one goal. Whether it was getting team members to read over the content over and over just so we get it right, or finding the solicitor to help go through the legal aspects or just having the moral support from friends and family, they all worked to get this book to the masses. We have a lot more in store for our consumers, not just our books as Money Luxury is inspired by everything and everyone around us, which we try to reciprocate by inspiring others, so thank you all also.

So to everyone mentioned, without you, this book would not be here today so much appreciation goes out to you all.

Much love and blessings.

Table of contents

CHAPTER 1 3

INTRODUCTION 3

WE ALL WANT MORE MONEY, RIGHT? 6

WHY THIS BOOK IS A GREAT READ? 8

HOW TO GENERATE AN EXTRA INCOME STREAM? 10

CHAPTER 2 13

WHAT IS TRADING? 13

KEY TERMS & WORDS 15

WHAT IS FOREX? 18

WHY TRADE FOREX? 20

HOW TO TRADE FOREX? 24

CHAPTER 3 30

TYPES OF MARKET ANALYSIS 30

CHART TYPES 33

TREND SPOTTING 35

INDICATORS & TOOLS 38

FIBONACCI 42

CHAPTER 4 46

THE THOUGHT PROCESS OF TRADING: THE PSYCHOLOGY	46
RISK MANAGEMENT	51
CONCLUSION	55
SPECIAL BONUS SECTION	58
THE MAJOR FX PAIRS & NICKNAMES	59
BROKERS TO PICK FROM	60
20 GREAT WEBSITES & SOURCES TO ASSIST YOU ON YOUR NEW JOURNEY	61
TOP 10 BOOKS ON TRADING & BUILDING WEALTH	62
13 GOLDEN TIPS FROM MONEY LUXURY	64

Chapter 1
INTRODUCTION

Hello to everyone reading this! Welcome to the *En Route To A Million* journey!

See what we did there? Anyway, first we want to say a big thank you for investing your time and hard earned money by buying and reading our first ever book here at Money Luxury. Taking a step toward bettering your financial situation – no matter how big or small – is a bold, yet very wise decision, because we believe someone who tries is already halfway there to achieving their dreams and aspirations.

At Money Luxury, we strive to inspire and motivate through our soon-to-be-published series of books, products and services, sharing our knowledge in acquiring wealth and achieving financial wellbeing. We have acquired this knowledge from our many years of thorough studying, experience of many highs and lows, and from continuous personal development, with a lot more to go as we still have not yet reached our ultimate goals.

We need you to understand that this is not a 'must follow' book or a 'guarantee' to make you money…let alone a millionaire; it's just an informative guidebook that could help you with the next step in your journey. It is also important to understand that even though our brand is 'Money Luxury' and we want to acquire wealth, at the end it's not all about the money. To be honest if we could just acquire the freedom money provides then we would not even care about money. So understand it is about having a passion, being free to do all the things you've always wanted to do and giving something back.

This is our first volume as we plan to publish more books to motivate and inspire people who invest in their future and aim to make a positive financial change in their lives. So if you enjoy the book, please do tell your friends and family so that we know we are doing something right.

Now, with no further ado! Here is the book many have been waiting for, what it is all about and why this could be the turning point in your life that you have been longing for!

Over the years the team at Money Luxury, individually as well as collectively, have wondered about ways to accumulate more money. This was because we were either tired of working a 9 to 5 job (you know what they say that means 'Just Over Broke'), never had any money once the monthly bills were paid, wanted to travel the world but unable to because our bank accounts were still in overdraft or we just simply wanted more income to be financially comfortable and free. So we all studied for a long time, various ways that we could become financially free, tried many different methods of making money, approaching many hurdles and many knock backs in the process. Through it all, one method that really stood out and was a common denominator for us; it caught our hearts like a beautiful model on the runway: 'Forex Trading'.

It was an industry that we studied over and over, which we took a while to grasp, as it may for many people, but now that you are reading this book, it shouldn't take you as long as it did us. It is the largest financial industry in terms of volume and traded an average of $5.3trillion per day in 2013 according to the Bank of International Settlements. This market is making more millionaires than ever before but also an industry that is making people broker than ever before. This is what we will be discussing in this book, hopefully gearing you up with the right equipment and armour to help you on your journey to a million.

So yes this book's main focus is forex! However this is not just a guide like any others you may have read; that may have fried your brains or filled your head with confusion regarding the technical terms, numbers and charts. This is a book that shares knowledge from over a combined 10 years of blood, sweat and tears studying the industry, and shares personal tips from experience, all crammed into this beautiful easy-to-read book just for you. Just to remind you that this is an informative guide not a guarantee to riches; so enjoy the read, take what you can and tell your friends all about it.

All the best for your journey!

WE ALL WANT MORE MONEY, RIGHT?

Yes! If you are reading this, your answer should be yes.

Having that extra bit of money can go a long way for many of us and it can get so frustrating when it seems not to click for you. The feeling of not being able to do the things you want to do or feel you should be doing; simple things like going on a vacation when you just need a break, paying bills that don't seem to be going away or just having the funds to pay for your driving lessons, yes driving lessons! This is a dream for some of us if we could do these things and the reason for us working our butts off to make ends meet.

It becomes very daunting when you feel like everything and everyone around you is moving forward but you seem to be in the same place day in and day out. We have all been there! It gets to a point that you are working so many hours that when you get home you are so tired that you don't even do the things you enjoy anymore. You begin to lose touch with your social life, family life and all you want is just some extra income to be able to be more flexible with your time and lifestyle. Right? Well, congratulations on making the decision to chase your dreams and aspirations by reading this guidebook.

For the financial situations listed above and many more, Money Luxury brings to you this book, full of insights and personal pointers that could steer you in the direction of living the life you want and deserve. We have tried our best to make sure it is all written in a clear cut and easy-to-read style; nonetheless bear in mind *this is not just an ordinary guidebook*, this is a book that really strives to inspire and motivate; it is divided into various sections that can guide you to and keep you on that right path if you understand and apply the knowledge it conveys.

So once again, the main focus of this book will be on the specific form of investing in your financial future; forex trading. While providing you with the technical aspects, we will also be providing you with key information on ways you could build the right character for this tough industry and life in general. *You know what they say: 'the hardest part isn't making the money, it's maintaining it'.*

Most of the contents of this book are from a real place, trial and error, and a lifetime of studying and sleepless nights, so understand it wasn't created overnight. Also in the same breath, note that this is merely just scraping the surface, so you will need to also do a lot more studying, research and will have to acquire your own experience into the trading industry.

WHY THIS BOOK IS A GREAT READ?

One key factor of this book is that it endeavours to boost your confidence and drive to believe that you could be 'en route to a million pounds' with the right amount of determination and passion. The team here at Money Luxury have included a valuable *Special Bonus Section*, a section that we spent a long time on, worked hard to put together and that we class as 'priceless information'. It is a section that encompasses team member's opinions, experiences and tips from the extensive tough journey to building wealth and it is all packed into just a few pages for you to take in and run with, if you want to. Not literally, obviously!

The bonus section is an additional section that we decided to throw in along with our insights and knowledge on the very lucrative and profitable forex industry. An industry you may have heard of before; probably tried to learn it after seeing an advert on YouTube or heard about that 18year old in the newspaper that spent £50,000 on champagne in a nightclub, yes £50,000! Even though this is very possible with forex, in order to get to that stage (if you are inclined to do so), it takes a lot of hard work, patience and discipline. The information in these pages is truly priceless, especially with features like our '13 Golden Tips from Money Luxury', 'Top 10 Books on trading and building wealth', 'Great websites to steer you in the right direction' and more. Go on, tell us, what other guidebook offers such great features?

En Route To A Million is a well thought out body of work created through years of learning about the industry which you could possibly learn in just a few hours, saving you from some painful sleepless nights, valuable time and money. Do understand as stated in our Disclaimer; do not take anything in our guidebook, website or resources *as a guaranteed ticket to riches* or *investment advice;* we are just sharing opinions, what has worked for us and other successful traders and we provide a general overview of the industry in question. Use what applies to you, your personality, style of living and trading.

Remember again, even though we have packed so much knowledge and tips into a wonderful book for you; nothing comes easy as we have had to experience ourselves, so you will need to do some additional reading and learning if you really want to achieve your goals as it won't all be within these pages. This extra studying will prove to be worth it!

HOW TO GENERATE AN EXTRA INCOME STREAM?

So, there are various ways to make more money in this land of opportunity that we live in. These include real estate, mobile applications, stocks, bonds, ISAs, setting up an online store, getting into the oil industry, selling unwanted goods, and working extra jobs. But we are here to focus on and tell you about *forex* trading. We believe it is a great form of investment and of making extra income, so buckle up for a wonderful and insightful ride…

Before we delve into the good stuff, it would be good for you to understand what you want, and to make it crystal clear to yourself! Whether it is a specific salary per year, or it is to buy your parents their dream home, or to buy a condo in Miami, or to make enough to pay regular bills and still have enough left over to treat yourself or simply to achieve the goal of being a MILLIONAIRE, which you'll be en route to if you continue to invest in yourself and remain focused on your goals.

Once this is clear in your mind, write it down somewhere where you can constantly look at it and review it! Then do something every day, small or big, to take you closer to these goals that you have written down. Even if you have to take a few minutes to do this now, if not done so already, it could help you a great deal.

Furthermore, it is important to do thorough *research* in any field before investing your money. If you are reading this, we're sure you know the importance of research and learning; this goes for everything you want to do in life. Before you get into an industry, it is beneficial if you learn the ins and outs and even once you've done that, continue to learn, research and develop in your field.

Once you understand that industry, know the risks involved and are confident of your ability to become successful; then *invest small* amounts of your money if you wish to, in the particular industry you have chosen. As most investments are a risk and could be a financial catastrophe if you are unprepared, make sure you invest amounts you can afford to lose just in the case your plans don't go your way. *You know what they say 'Never put all your eggs in one basket'*: quite cliché but it is such a wise phrase and will prove crucially important on your journey to wealth.

When you have found a proven method that works for you consistently in that industry, it fits around your lifestyle and personality, just repeat the same process and then you can consider implementing a famous method of building wealth called *compounding*. This is something that we will discuss a little later on; but it is a great way to increase your income stream.

So yes, those are our key tips on making extra income...hope you're learning something!

Now this is where the journey of forex trading starts...

Chapter 2
WHAT IS TRADING?

'Trading' generally implies an exchange of one item or product for another. Trading in regard to what we will be exploring in this book is 'forex', otherwise known as the foreign exchange market or FX. This market is the largest financial market and is based on speculation and predicting the movement of prices in relation to various currencies around the world. So 'trading' comes into play here because people buy and sell currencies to and from each other in the world of forex, not personally but through a decentralized financial market, the foreign exchange.

As you may know or have experienced that when you travel to another country, you would need to change your currency to the currency of the country you have travelled to. So what happens in this case is that you have sold your home currency and bought the new currency, so technically this is a trade.

Before anyone, anywhere in the world with Internet access were able to trade online, the only form of trading was electronic trading between the banks and financial establishments, which is no longer the only way to trade. Many years ago a genius came up with the idea to make it accessible for individual investors who wanted to make extra money to be able to predict whether the price of a currency pair will go up or down, another way of saying this is a currency pair being *bullish* or *bearish*. Bullish implies an upward trend, while bearish implies a downward trend.

Yes this market does make you money, correct! But it is not as simple as it may sound or look to many of you and just to make you aware, there are many types of trading or financial instruments which can be traded online, such as commodities, stocks, indexes and many others. You not need worry about the majority of the above now as the focus will be solely on currency trading, in particular forex.

The financial industry is a broad spectrum as even within the currency market there are different types of trading, for example binary options, also known as spot trading. This form of trading is similar to forex but also very different. Instead of accumulating pips/points or trading with a spread like forex, you predict if the price will be more or less than the current price at a particular time.

So, back to the topic at hand, here is an example of what you can trade in the forex market. Although many brokers offer the opportunity to trade commodities and indexes, the main instruments are currency pairs also known as symbols. One popular example is the Great British Pound and the Dollar (known as GBP/USD) and these are two currencies being paired against each other, one of the major pairs that traders look at and trade. It is important to know that the first currency in a FX pair that is quoted is known as the *base* currency (in this case

GBP) and the second quoted is the *counter* currency. When reading the price of a currency pair, it shows how much of the counter currency is needed to get the base currency (which is valued at one unit).

KEY TERMS & WORDS

Here is a list of key terms that traders constantly use and that you may hear a lot in the rest of the book. So to save you from thinking what the hell is going on! ...every few minutes, we thought we would enlighten you beforehand about all the fancy words and give you their brief trading definitions! After reading these, you're going to start feeling and thinking more like a trader already! Well done!

Bearish – when a trend or market is going down
Bias – this is related to a trader's prediction of price action or a trend
Bullish – when a trend or market is going up
Breakouts – when the price has moved past a particular key level of support or resistance
Candlestick – the bar shapes on a financial chart that has two needles at each end; this formation shows the opening, the closing, the highest and the lowest price over a given time period
Channels – usually are the parallel lines connecting prices, previous highs and lows

Confluence – a number of things to add to a particular prediction
Downtrend – when the price of a currency pair or financial instrument is going down, making lower highs and lower lows
Economic Calendar – where live news data is displayed with results of past and current data (a key factor in the trading industry)
Equity – the total amount in a trading account, this amount of money is what a trader can trade with
Extension – this is used with the Fibonacci tool, three points are placed on the chart to gauge where the price may reach
Fibonacci – this is a number sequence, containing a series of numbers, which are found by adding the previous two numbers e.g. 1, 1, 2, 3, 5, 8
Floors – the next key level up or down from current price level
Intraday trader – a type of trader that buys and sells a particular financial instrument within the same trading day
Leverage – this is related to borrowing specific sums of money from a broker to be able to invest and place trades in forex
Margin – this is the total amount of equity a trader is required to have in order to invest
Pips – the smallest unit a currency's exchange rate can make; also known as points and is usually displayed as the fourth decimal place
Resistance – a key level that price has had difficulty rising above

Retracement – this is related to the Fibonacci tool, two points that are placed on a chart to gauge where price may draw back to before continuing its original trend
Reversal – this is when a trend has changed its predominant direction and starts going the opposite way
Signals – these are catalysts that help traders gauge the right direction of price action
Spinning tops – a particular candlestick formation showing a trend; it is regarded to be neutral
Spread – this is the difference between the buying and selling price and the amount that the broker takes once you place a trade
Stop-loss order – this is an order with a broker and the price limit a trader is willing to go when losing in a trade; used to manage risk
Support – a key level that price has had difficulty falling below
Swing trader – a type of trader that focuses on trading long term, buying and selling financial instruments longer than a day
Take profit – this is the opposite of a stop-loss, so it is an order with a broker and the price limit a trader is willing to go to when winning in a trade
Trend lines – this is a technical analysis formation that traders draw on a chart; to indicate rising or falling key levels
Uptrend – when the price of a currency pair or financial instrument is going up, making higher highs and higher lows
Volatility – when a financial instrument can be seen to move up and down frequently in a short period

WHAT IS FOREX?

(This image sums up what the trading journey looks like)

Forex is the largest financial market, one that trades currency worth over 4 trillion USD every day. This makes it easier for countries to trade goods internationally and retail investors to trade currencies with other traders through a decentralized hub that is open 24 hours a day (except for the weekends). Also this is a market that provides great opportunities for people outside the big financial companies and banks to make money while the prices of currencies fluctuate since the development of the Internet. Again, in this financial market, forex is another word for foreign exchange.

The main financial trading centres around the world are New York, London,

FOREX MARKET CENTRE	TIME ZONE	OPENS US/Eastern	CLOSES US/Eastern
Frankfurt Germany	Europe/Berlin	2:00 AM 15-February-2016	10:00 AM 15-February-2016
London Great Britain	Europe/London	3:00 AM 15-February-2016	11:00 AM 15-February-2016
New York United States	America/New York	8:00 AM 15-February-2016	4:00 PM 15-February-2016
Sydney Australia	Australia/Sydney	4:00 PM 14-February-2016	12:00 AM 15-February-2016
Tokyo Japan	Asia/Tokyo	6:00 PM 14-February-2016	2:00 AM 15-February-2016

Hong Kong, Tokyo, Sydney, and Frankfurt. The market opens and closes at different times around the world because of the different time zones, which is why it is a 24 hour market. Trading begins at 20:00 GMT on a Sunday and closes and 22:00 GMT on a Friday. The image on the left is a table of the different trading sessions to give you a clearer picture.

As the speed of the Internet has increased rapidly over the years it has made it accessible and facilitated individual investors who want to get into forex trading. This is why we are so lucky to be alive right now, as we are living in The Information Age, which means we have instant access to almost everything we can think of due to the Internet and the rapid development of technology. Really, as hard as it may feel to make money, there is no excuse not to! It is much easier said than done and the truth hurts, but it's true!

The likes of Google and YouTube have made it possible for people to become millionaires from their bedrooms. Great right? Well forex is one of those things that gave many people the title *bedroom millionaires* and it is accessible for anyone as long as you are of age and have access to the Internet. Brokers have made it even easier for people to get into the industry by offering competitive features on their platforms, such as free demo trading, tight spreads, access to live currency prices and access to live news data, which we will discuss soon.

(This here is a picture of some of the major currency pairs; Source: City Index)

WHY TRADE FOREX?

Different people have different reasons to get into forex trading; one key reason is that it is a viable avenue and great opportunity to become financially free! It is as simple as that! Some people want to trade forex to earn money, some want to learn a new skill, some love mathematics and others may be interested in it for the thrill it gives them. Whatever your reason is for wanting to trade forex, allow it to change you for the better, have fun and be smart with it and try not to let it change you for the worse! Forex is a place that you can make unlimited amounts of money; it has become very popular in the past decade because it offers traders several advantages, which we will be touching on below.

DEMO ACCOUNTS
The good thing about forex is that you don't have to start with your own money to learn to trade. You can use one of many of the free demo accounts that brokers have provided for individual investors to use for absolutely nothing. Demo accounts contain up to several thousand artificial pounds and are a great way to learn and develop a strategy. It is also a great way to test your discipline as many people get carried away when they see large amounts of money and think they can win big. The best thing you can do when you start demo trading or if you are already using a demo; is be realistic with your trades, as though it were your own money. It would be pointless if you did not consider and implement risk management just because it is a demo and think you would be ready for a live account as you would most probably lose in an instant because of the bad habit you acquired from trading in your demo account. So take advantage of the fact that you can learn about the industry with live data, trading free of charge, but also try to remain realistic.

24 HOUR TRADING
In the world of forex the great thing about it is that you can trade at any time of the day, as the markets are open 24 hours a day,

excluding weekends. There are three key regions that the market is made up of: Europe, North America and Australasia which at times overlap in regard to their trading sessions. The reason for 24 hour trading is that currency trading is not traded at a particular physical location and also because many countries around the world also trade for international exchanges, so the market is open during the specific business hours of those countries. For example, the business hours in the UK are generally 9am until 5pm (GMT) and this is generally where the market will be the most volatile in the UK, so this is a good time to trade. Being able to trade at any time, unlike other financial markets, proves to be very beneficial for traders as there is a greater opportunity to make money.

FLEXIBILITY
One of the advantages of getting into this industry is that the time you commit to trading is flexible and unlimited. The amount of trading one does is entirely up to that person; this is where different personalities and lifestyles will come into play. If you are someone who has a lot of other things going on in your life, like a full time job, family, kids, or if you participate in many different activities then you may not want to be at your computer every day, placing many trades and accumulating small pip gains on the charts. You may prefer to place a trade and let it run for a few days or even longer; this type of trading is done by a long-term trader, also known as a swing or trend trader. Trading forex allows you to have a life and you can always trade wherever you are in the

world as long as you have access to the internet…isn't that great?

LOW TRADING COSTS

As stated earlier, many forex platforms have become easily accessible and available for traders; novices and experts. This has produced tremendous competition within the industry, so companies are constantly trying to find new ways of appealing to traders. The cost of trading is very low as many brokers allow you to fund a live account with 50GBP or even less, which can help you manage risk. They usually have an opportunity for people to trade on a demo account with substantial amounts of money and have tight spreads to entice people to use their platform. This also enables you to trade live currency prices, which provide traders with a great sense of familiarity and understanding of how the industry works while enabling you to use the indicators, tools and live data feeds to assist trading.

LEVERAGING

Being able to leverage in this industry is one of the major benefits that assists investors to trade and benefit from the large trading volumes in forex. Leveraging is based on margin requirements and the leverage offered will differ depending on the broker you use and this can vary on average from 50:1 to 400:1. A forex trader has the opportunity to trade with a large leverage, which could ultimately allow them to make a large profit from small moves in price action. It is important to understand that even though it allows room to make large profits, leveraging also allows room for major financial losses, therefore risk management is a key factor here.

HOW TO TRADE FOREX?

This is the 'Money Luxury' way to trade forex, and as stated earlier this is not your typical guidebook; this is more of an insight into the diaries of traders who have studied the industry thoroughly. So in this sub chapter, it is more about a few things that could equip you for battle rather than the basic just 'buy low, sell high' lines you may have heard at a trading seminar that you paid £2000 for at the end of the talk.

You may be wondering; why the term *battle*? It was deliberately used, because we like to visualise the market as exactly that…a battle! We believe that you will need to see your en route to a million journey as a battle going into this industry as well as in life in general, because let's face it – it's tough out there! So try to understand that this is what it is like, each time to you step into those charts, a battlefield!

Trading forex is closely related to and can be seen as a war between traders and the market; this is because the market can be very nasty and vicious if you don't take the necessary precautions, a mistake many traders make. Maybe because the charts look so innocent and pretty at times that you do not think they could do any harm…right? Just green and red bars going up and down with a few colourful lines through them; well the reality is that these colourful-looking things are ruining the lives of people who don't take them seriously and are not fully equipped to handle them. So, treat them very seriously! Like something that you will need to be well trained in and educated in, just like in a career!

The best example of the market destroying lives and wreaking havoc is the 2008 economic crash! Many investors did not anticipate that the financial market would dip a few thousand points in such a short time. Many may have not been cautious enough to have a stop loss in place, which resulted in their trading accounts being wiped out completely. Those that did not know about financial planning could have had their life savings in one account. You can imagine the drastic consequences of losing your life savings; many people lost their partners of many years, many lost their homes and even many even lost their lives after the crash. So basically it was total bloodshed!

Now you can see why we say that it is important to be equipped, do your research, use correct risk management and maintain discipline. We are not trying to scare you, just want to point out the severity of not taking the correct precautions of being a trader.

One of the key aims of writing this book is to offer some weapons for your arsenal or even body armour that you may need. Like we stated before you will need to get more equipment from other sources to complete your armour for battle; all of it won't be in this book alone, this is just a fraction. So here is some of your equipment listed below and like everything we offer... take it or leave it!

Create A Trade Journal

One thing we noticed in our trading journey, that it was a key advantage to 'journal' the activities and the process along the way. It is a habit that could help and assist in building the right character, consistency and discipline; especially if you note down all your *observations* and *mistakes* for each trade made. Writing down your trades, what you have witnessed in the market, your predictions and areas where you are going wrong can help you understand the areas you need to improve each step of the way and understand what is going on in the financial industry. Creating a trading journal also helps when you need to analyse and look back on the history of currency prices and what it has done before, as they say in this industry *'history always repeats itself'*. So it is always important to see what has happened previously to help anticipate what may happen in the future.

Start With A Demo Account

When starting your trading journey and from the first trade you ever place we believe that you should start on a demo account. Understand how the charts move, *practice* and test your strategy until you are consistently making money. Once you are comfortable with trading and understand the main factors of trading forex, you should move to a personal account but start with an amount you can afford to lose. Use the demo account to get familiar with trying and testing different indicators, timeframes and tools to trade, which will all be key factors in your trading.

(Build a strategy that enables you financial freedom)

Always Remain Disciplined
It is very important, especially for new traders, to maintain *DISCIPLINE* and be consistent at all times. This is because if you lose discipline, you are more vulnerable to failure, which can cause a domino effect on

your finances, your wellbeing and your life in general. It is crucial to have self-control and to never bring your emotions to the market. An emotional trader loses focus and control as they are so caught up in their feelings that they make drastic decisions, ones that they may not usually make if they were in a stable frame of mind.

We have all made this mistake before; when we set our mind on a particular trade, assuming we are totally right so we place the trade, possibly increase the stake because we feel so confident. Only to return to the trade a few hours later and realise we have lost money. In this period, you are so shocked that the market has taken your money when you totally believed you made the right prediction, you now want your money back as soon as possible. So you place another trade, just to gain the loss back, and this is where emotional trading comes in! Not sitting down to plan or analyse! Now after everything is said and done, you lose more than intended, more than the daily limit and then have eventually blown your whole account. This is a regular occurrence in the trading world and very easy to get dragged into, so if you can learn to remain disciplined from the start and keep it up, then you will go far in the industry.

Build A Strategy
It is important to develop a *routine* and a *strategy* that you can always follow for trading. This strategy can contain various factors, such as the time of day you decide to trade, what currency pairs you trade, how long

you leave trades on, types of analysis you use or even the type of indicators you decide to use to assist your decision making. Everyone is different and will prefer different ways of doing things, so a strategy that works for someone else may not necessarily work for you. We will discuss more about strategies a little later and in more detail, explaining specific ways to develop a strategy that suits you.

When you have found your strategy you may realise that you find different reasons to enter a trade or new forms of market analysis, this is fine, keep your mind open to new techniques as this could benefit you. Tweaking your strategy is a normal thing to do when trading… but you know what they say, *'if it is not broken then don't fix it';* so do consider this saying when thinking about tweaking your strategy.

CHAPTER 3
TYPES OF MARKET ANALYSIS

There are three main types of market analysis in forex trading which we believe all work together and are all important factors to consider. It is a great idea to check on the charts *regularly* to see how price action is playing out and to get familiar with your favourite currency pairs, even when you do not place a trade. This proves beneficial for us at Money Luxury because many times we have missed major moves, have left trades unattended for many hours or even days to notice that the market has unexpectedly deviated from the norm or gone against us. This does not mean check your trades every minute, but depending on your style, it is good to keep an eye on what is happening in the charts, and on the market in general, especially if your money is on the line.

Always check yearly performances and see what factors drive the market, such as interest rates, politics, speeches, wars, current affairs, major endorsements and global news. It has been said many times on this trading journey that *'Fear and Greed'* drive the market, so that is something to consider and is greatly related to the first type of analysis that we will be discussing below.

Sentimental Analysis
This type of analysis is based on ideologies and actions of individual traders created by looking at price action or because traders may feel that the price is overvalued; so basically these are just opinions. The forex market is driven by people and what drives people in these markets is fear and greed. This information can help you as a trader to gauge where price may go if you understand how to get a feel for what other traders are feeling and thinking at a given time period. For example, if a trend is an uptrend, this shows the bulls are confident, so the general feeling of traders is bullish. So you can use this information to help assist your trading decisions as well as other factors for a more refined bias and added confluence.

Fundamental Analysis
Getting information from news and economic data from unique sources will assist you with your trading predictions, as you will be more likely to correctly predetermine the outcome based on a particular news event or data release. It is advisable to do your own thorough research and spend hours finding the right sources to guide you in this area. News is used as a catalyst to complement your trading bias, so

for example if your prediction and analysis tells you to sell a currency pair and a major news announcement relating to this particular currency pair comes out which is negative, then that has made your bias or prediction more likely. Get it? See how you need to piece bits together like a puzzle before you actually make any trades, it's not just rushing and going off impulse; it is more pre planned and thought out!

(Image: Live Data feed; Source: City Index)

Technical Analysis

This form of analysis is the best for us here at Money Luxury, the reason being it is a more accurate form of analysis, compared to the others. With technicals, you begin to make predictions due to calculations, signals and tools, which we will be discussing further on in the book. This is mainly where tools such as Fibonacci, moving averages, trend lines, channels and many others come into play. We love technicals, because the majority of the time, if you correctly place your technicals and use the right tools, you can correctly gauge the direction of the price and when it may make a reversal or even a continuation. Sounds very technical? Don't worry, we have all been there, you will get it soon!

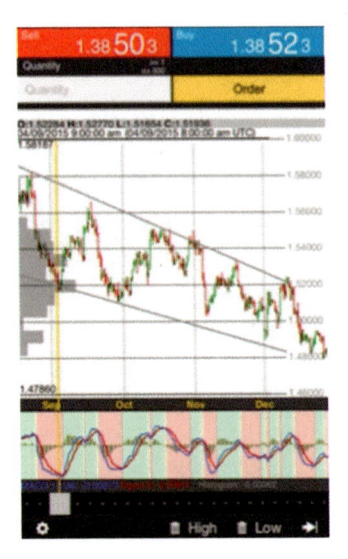

(Image of technicals being used to analyse a chart; Source: City Index)

CHART TYPES

Line chart
This is a type of graph in forex that is not used as much as before. It is a line that shows price action. Line charts resemble moving average lines as it is just one line to show the momentum of price over a particular period.

Candlestick chart
This is the commonly used Japanese candlesticks; invented by a famous Japanese trader many years ago. Candlestick charts are great because they give you a lot

of information such as the lowest point the price has gone, the highest, when price opened and closed all within a particular time. These periods could be 1minute, 1hour, 4hours, daily, weekly or monthly. *(If you would like to understand more about the different candlestick formations then check out our website for more information: www.moneyluxury.co.uk)*

Bar chart
These are quite similar to candlesticks but they don't have wicks. This form of chart shows when price opened and when it closed and was the most popular a few years back before the candlestick was invented.

(Line chart)   *(Candlestick Chart)*   *(Bar chart)*
(Images Source: City Index)

TREND SPOTTING

Being able to spot a trend or a particular type of pattern instantly will really help you when trading. When looking at a chart you should be able to say which direction the trend is in, whether it is an uptrend, downtrend or a range, within the first few seconds. This will help and train you to spot what's going in the charts more effectively and accurately; it's almost like having the eye of a tiger, being able to spot types of waves, retracement levels, etc. as this will make you a more confident and efficient trader, which will ultimately help you make profits from the market. There are many types of chart patterns and a few main types of trends with ways in which you can mark them (trend lines) as we see in the image on the right. We will explain briefly a few different types of patterns that are mainly traded.

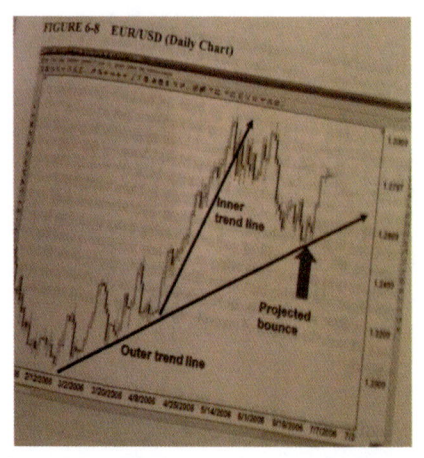

Image above: Trend lines drawn on a EUR/USD chart; 10 Essentials of Forex Trading

ABCD Pattern
This pattern is formed from the Fibonacci retracement and extension levels, which occur at particular price points; a pattern that contains four legs: A through to D. An example of how it is formed is, from the starting point of the BC leg, the price must retrace to one of the Fib levels; .618 or .786 then continue in the main trend direction, completing the ABCD formation. These legs are usually the same in length, which is a good indicator to let you know what type of chart pattern has formed, leading you to make a more informed decision with your trade.

Wave patterns
This is another type of chart pattern that traders are always on the lookout for and is based on the famous Elliot Wave theory. Ralph Nelson Elliot pioneered this chart pattern and it was named after him; this pattern is related to trends that are confluent with the main trend direction. There are two types of waves: the impulse wave and correction wave. The wave pattern can be found on various timeframes, which makes it a pattern that many traders use to assist their trading as it builds confidence knowing the pattern is very consistent in the forex industry.

Gartley Pattern
Another pattern formed around the Fibonacci levels; now you can see why we speak so highly of Fibonacci and even dedicated a whole sub chapter to the famous

tool. The Gartley was created by a man called Mr Harold M. Gartley; who came up with a great theory that helped a trader to distinguish when the price of a currency pair would go up or down at a particular point in the chart. This pattern measures price retracements and speculates when the trend is making a reversal.

Channel
This is a market trend and term that indicates to traders the type of trend that a currency pair is in from its consecutive swing lows and highs. Traders look for this pattern during their technical analysis and it is a great way to assist in determining what direction the price will go in next; if it is due for a retracement or along with possible indicators that its tired and due for a reversal. So if you see a currency pair that is making higher highs and higher lows, the trend is in an uptrend, so you would keep an eye out for buying opportunities. Similarly if you see a trend that is making lower lows then that tells you that the market is in a downtrend and you would look for selling opportunities; forming the channel pattern.

Seeing any trend pattern or formation, does not mean that it will always go in that direction and that you are always right! You may need to use this with other information e.g. indicators, news etc. to have a high probability trade.

(This is GBP/USD forming a Channel pattern; Source: City Index)

INDICATORS & TOOLS

In the world of forex, many fancy tools can assist one's trading decisions and they are used to add confluence to your general predictions. The best way to use these is not to solely depend on them but to use them as a catalyst, increasing the probability of a trade going in your direction. The different indicators and tools can all be used and altered to different timeframes, which is an advantage for different types of traders.

One thing we would say about them is to test the waters and see which indicator you most prefer; from there you should focus on using that one or two tools and become an expert in using them. You do not want to be overwhelmed by using so many different indicators, making your trading journey more difficult than it needs to be.

Many people have the misconception that the best traders use every tool, adding different lines and shapes to the charts but what we have realised and learnt is that 'keeping it simple is the most effective way' in trading. Here is a list of some of the main tools you can use. There are several more, which you will need to do independent research on, so pick your favourite and remember to keep it simple!

MACD

The MACD stands for Moving Average Convergence Divergence created by a man named Gerald Appel. It was developed and mainly used for gauging trend momentum; visually showing the relationship between moving averages formed over particular time periods. The MACD is an oscillator, which can show the frequency of a trend moving up and down past the zero mark as the moving average lines converge and diverge. Traders use it by looking for crossovers of the lines to the down or upside and look

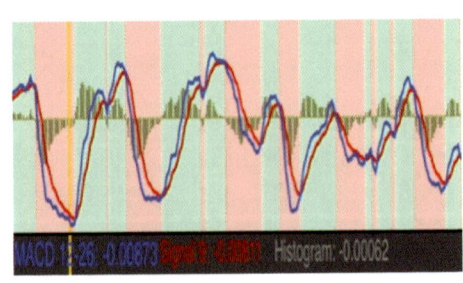

where the ends of the lines are pointing to have a clearer understanding of what price is doing.
The oscillator is like a bar graph that shows various bars, different in length and as they get shorter and taller traders also use this to gauge what price might be doing. The general time periods that are used for the MACD lines are 12, 26 and 9, but this is subject to choice and how you would like to trade. It is a good idea not only with this indicator but all the ones you explore, to try different settings and time periods for each and find what one works for you and what one you understand best.

Image above; Source: City Index

Moving Averages (MAs)
This is an indicator that is used by many traders for the extra support of their bias on a trend and its actions. It is based on historical prices, which can be altered to your needs and is made to allow traders to view the trend in a much simpler way as it is a single line that eliminates the choppiness of a currency pair that fluctuates constantly. The EMA and the SMA are the two widely used MAs by traders, tailored to suit their style of trading and are usually used for following trends and identifying the key levels on a chart.

RSI
This indicator stands for Relative Strength Index and is another favourite of the traders. Members of the team at Money Luxury like to use this one as well, as it is good

for signalling when a trend has become either undersold or overbought. It shows a range of 0 – 100, with the 30, 50 and 70 mark also visible and this is where the RSI line fluctuates. The RSI is an average of the last specific amount of time periods formed as a single line and once it begins to dip below the 30 mark, this indicates to traders that it is becoming oversold so it prompts to look for opportunities to buy. On the other hand when the RSI begins to rally above the 70 mark, this tells traders that they may need to start selling soon as the price may be overbought at that particular time.

Ichimoku Cloud
A Japanese journalist, Goichi Hosoda created this indicator for technical analysts to indicate the key levels of support and resistance on a trading chart, also showing the direction in which a trend is going and its momentum similar to the MAs we spoke of earlier. These are combined to create the Ichimoku cloud and the good thing about this indicator is that it can give an instant visual and show what is happening during a particular time frame once you get used to using it regularly. Traders can form their bias from the MAs in this indicator as they signal downtrends when one line crosses over to the downside and likewise if a line crosses over to the upside, it's a great possibility that the trend is becoming bullish. These lines are called the 'Tenkansen' and the 'Kijun-sen', which create a span also known as the 'cloud' when they diverge and converge. Also when the price is quite a few points above the cloud, the bulls usually look for opportunities

to buy and vice versa if the price is a few points below the cloud then the bears look for opportunities to sell.

FIBONACCI

The word 'Fibonacci' is used in almost every sentence in the trading world and it is the reason many people make profits from the industry. This fancy term originates from a famous Italian mathematical genius, named Leonardo Fibonacci. His theory and discovery goes to show that the market does not just do whatever it likes or pleases and that even we as humans are created in a numerical sequence, which we will outline shortly. Understanding how to use this tool can be the much needed and awaited turning point in a person's trading career.

So just to make clear, Fibonacci is a numerical sequence used by many forex traders to predict the price of a currency pair. This is done by marking key levels, retracement levels and extension levels.

A bit of history, ahem! Class in session! Leonardo Fibonacci was born in Italy in 1170 and educated in North Africa. He travelled with his dad to different countries and on one of his journeys, he discovered the Fibonacci sequence because he began to gradually recognize the enormous advantages of the mathematical systems of the countries they were visiting versus the

Roman numerals he had been taught. One of the mathematical concepts that intrigued Fibonacci was the nine-digit system (1, 2, 3, 4, 5, 6, 7, 8, 9) used by the Indians. So when he returned home he started to work with the royal families introducing the numbers 0 through 9. In the early 1200s he wrote many texts on maths and his theories, which you can research and read all about.

So the famous Fibonacci was fascinated by numbers and he discovered this numerical sequence, *the sum of the previous two numbers will always equal the next number in the sequence*. Check it out...

1, 2, 3, 5, 8, 13, 21, 34, to infinity

The fascinating part of this is that nature is closely related to the Fibonacci sequence; for example rabbits multiply in the Fibonacci sequence, pineapple scales grow in a numerical sequence and even sunflower seeds grow in numerical sequence. This finding proved that they are mathematical numerical sequences in many places in the world and in nature.

(Fibonacci Retracement Levels on the EUR/GBP pair; Source: City Index)

FIGURE 8-10 Fibonacci Sequence in the Human Face

Ratios in the Face

- Eyes are at the 0.382
- Ears and nose are at the 0.50
- Mouth is at the 0.786

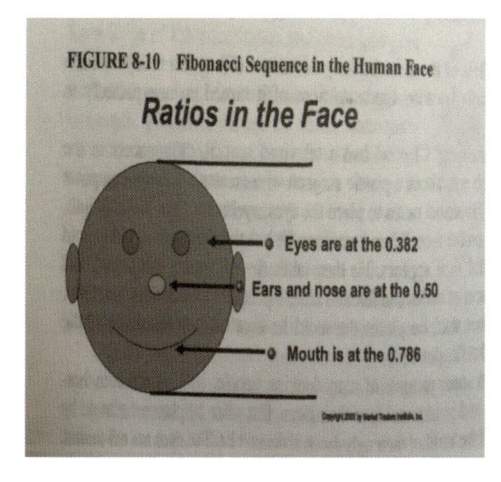

(Fibonacci sequence in the human face; 10 Essentials of Forex Trading)

Hope you are learning something and enjoying the journey so far…

CHAPTER 4
THE THOUGHT PROCESS OF TRADING: THE PSYCHOLOGY

So that's it for the technical jargon, you can let your brain relax a little now! At Money Luxury, we believe that trading is based more on psychology than skill. As it is quite easy to read and learn something if you do it many times, but if you've learnt something and have not grasped a particular mind set related to what you have learnt, then it becomes irrelevant.

As a trader it is important to train your mind to have a consistent thought process and we will be discussing a few things that can assist you with this crucial goal. Again this is one of the great things about our book; these are key tips to become successful, tips we took a long time to come up with, through years of making mistakes and note taking; so if you like what you read, take it and use it! Enjoy…

One important habit in forex and life in general is exercising *self-control* and having *patience*. These are key factors and major characteristics that are needed to be a successful trader, it's like waiting for a bus; another setup will come in five minutes (well probably longer but you get the drift). So knowing this information, to be a successful trader you will need to be able to sit on your hands a lot of the time.

A key habit that was very helpful to us was making *predictions* or paper trades every so often. This is based on deciding where you think the price will go and why, noting it down and then reviewing results with personal feedback and pointers (at least a couple trades a day). This helps with your mind frame on the industry because the more you do this the better you get, the more you learn and the more confident you are. When a person is confident, good things usually happen to them and in this case your trading improves and that equates to more money. Great, right?

When starting out, it is important to understand that the money will come, but not straight away. It is easy to get carried away because you get so excited to start this new forex journey and want to make so much money right away, but it cannot work like that. You have to start slow and steady; one way this was done was to *prove* to ourselves that we could catch *pips* and not the money. Understand that pips make the money, so if you can consistently catch pips then the money will follow. Do not get greedy; learn your craft before you focus on the money.

Do *tests* and exercises to stimulate the brain every now and then. This is a great tactic to put you in the frame of mind of thinking that this is not a joke and that you need to revise, research and train for forex; for example set yourself 10 questions to answer…almost like an exam when you were in college. The thing about trading is that because it is such an independent form of making money, people can easily become complacent and because nobody is there to say 'study hard', they develop bad habits which could later affect them, so don't take the risk. Constantly give yourself a test, this could be once a week or once a month or more, it's all up to you.

Understand and constantly remind yourself that *emotions* should *never* be brought to the trading table ever! This is one of the key rules when trading and has been emphasized by many top traders and professional finance managers. Many people fail in the forex industry because they get emotionally attached to their trades. When you bring emotions to the table, you are not making informed decisions based on facts and logic, so this increases the likelihood of you losing your trade. Learn to leave your emotions at the door so to speak; so this means not getting angry, shocked, upset, overexcited and not falling in love with any charts or currency pairs. Even though you may have favourite pairs that you enjoy trading, try your best not to get attached as they can break your heart if you are not careful.

Watch videos, tutorials, read books on discipline and spend hours *motivating* yourself. This will help you to mentally train and equip yourself for whatever comes your way in the trading realm. This is one of the main areas where you will need to take responsibility for your own development; because it is key and no one will help you if you don't help yourself. As we live in this great era of The Information Age, there are many resources to help with motivation and discipline, many professionals and self-made millionaires have spoken on these topics, which are available for anyone to access.

Live for today, hope for tomorrow is something we like to use to keep focused. This means live in the moment, don't dwell on the past as that has passed so hope for the best and have faith that tomorrow will be a better day for yourself and your trading. You can even use this in your general day-to-day life, as it helps with your thought process on a continuous basis. I'm sure you have heard before that the mind is a powerful tool; everything starts there. So your thinking determines the actions you take in your life and if you are constantly worrying or dwelling on what happened to you yesterday then you're going to let it affect your tomorrow and the actions you take. So always stay positive.

A habit of ours is to always reflect and look at our *goals* and aims to see where we are and to remind ourselves of where we need to be. This is done to keep on track, almost like a guideline and to make aware of how much has been achieved, ultimately understanding what else needs to be done to reach the goals set. Doing a goal review at least once a week or month should be enough to keep one going. It is a routine that proves to be very helpful in having the right mind set because sometimes you may go off track and need that extra push to get you back on the right path. It is very crucial to remember why you started and refer to the drawing board because it happens to many of us; we begin to make profit or even lose then we begin to forget the core reason for starting in the first place. Remembering why you started can create a sense of realism and humility when trading, which is important. So if you have not done so already, start creating a goals list and achieve them with no question in mind.

The final tip for building a strong mind frame and psychology is understanding and constantly reminding yourself; making it an unconscious habit to *never give up!* No matter how hard it begins to feel or how much it hurts, you are going to have many times on your route to a million, where you just want to throw in the towel, you even make up your mind that you are going to stop trying because it is starting to take a toll on you; but you need to snap out of that thought process as soon as possible and remember that you came so far now, and there is no point turning back. There have been days when we've spent whole nights without sleeping, trying to crack our brain on how to read charts, how to use indicators and tools but still not getting anywhere. At that point the feeling of wanting to give up is so strong but then we remember that we have resolved to ourselves that we will 'never give up' until the wheels fall off. You will eventually reap your rewards just stick in there and keep pushing until you have reached your goals.

So that's our list of tips to assist you in getting in the right frame of mind for this tough industry, we believe these points helped and is still helping us on our journey. You can always add or subtract, to create your own list but understand that it takes a lot of practice and consistency to achieve these goals because to have the right psychology, you need to build unconscious habits, which takes time.

RISK MANAGEMENT

Now please understand that if there's only one thing that you want to take from this book (hopefully there's more), but yes if it is only one thing then let it be *'Risk Management'*. This is a key difference between a good and a bad trader. If you make a profit from a trade but your risk management was not solid then we will still class it as a bad trade and vice versa if you lose your money but your risk management was solid then we will call it a good trade, do you see where we are heading with this? Great!

It is important to stick to a set rule regarding your risk and your risk-to-reward ratio, which allows you to accumulate more money than you would if you lost. One ratio and rule we follow here at Money Luxury is 'Never risk more than 2% of our total account on any given trade, have a risk/reward ratio of at least 1:2, 1:3 is better' and 'Never lose more than 5% on any given day'. This is an example of following a system to enable good risk management, you can use this or amend it to suit your needs. Bear in mind that 5% is a personal limit but many professionals say do not risk more than 1%, but it all comes down to personal preference at the end of the day.

Please do understand that risk management is another (if not the most important) factor to being successful in forex trading. So here are a few points that could assist you:

Protect yourself 24/7 in relation to risk management; it is a crucial and important factor to successful trading, as this helps ensure that you do not lose all your money so fast or not even at all. You can protect yourself by always placing a *stop loss* on each trade, which in our case, would not exceed 2% on any given trade. So for example, when placing a trade (this may sound complicated and not clear just yet to some) you could make your stop loss relative to the previous *resistance* or *support* levels, which should not exceed your 2% limit and not only just based on how much you're willing to lose, the trade must make sense to have a higher chance of a winning trade.

It is always good to have in mind how much you want to make in a day, a week or a month so that you can also fit your strategy around this *target*. This could be in terms of pips or money, just have a set amount or limit that you want to achieve each trade, this could be for the day, week or month depending on your trading strategy and style but should be kept realistic. Below we have given an example of how you may work out your risk management with all the above being considered on an account of £1000.

(Example of risk management for an account with the total equity £1000)

Starting account balance of £1000:

This is an account of a day trader called Ben, and the maximum he is willing to lose on each day is a total amount of 5% so that is £50. This limit could apply to either one trade or various trades but the total loss cannot exceed more than his £50 limit per day, with a target of £150 profit (Risk-to-reward of 1:3).

If Ben places one trade for the day with a stake of £1 per pip, a risk-to-reward ratio of 1:3 then he intends to make £150 for that trade which also fits his pip target (50:150pips at £1 per PIP).

In order for his strategy and risk management to go as planned, he will need to find a chart and setup that can work around his risk management and aims, taking into consideration the type of trend, where the previous highs and lows are and his probability of success.

Hope you've understood how to manage risk a little better and how to implement this on the charts…

CONCLUSION

So now we are getting closer to the end of your guidebook and your first journey with us! Don't worry there are still more great pointers to be given to you all out there and still to come our *'Special Bonus'* section. This part of the book is going to be more of a round-up of what we have discussed so far and things you need to remember as they will be handy once you have left us.

Remember that everything in this book is personal experience, turned into an insight for others; it does not have to be replicated. So use your own discretion regarding what we have discussed; you have to understand that it is going to be a personal journey, with personal goals and personal aims, so in order to achieve success you will need to find out what works for you personally. We will be discussing how you can take notes and journal the process, and like we said we would, we will help you to implement a routine that will help you get into a productive habit.

Having a strategy is like a personal holy grail that you need to follow no matter what the situation is at hand. It needs to be well thought out and a plan that suits you, that compliments your personality and works around the time you have available to dedicate to your trading. Once it feels like a good strategy has been created, test it repeatedly to see how successful it is and once proven to work consistently and is majority of the time successful, follow that strategy if you think it is right for you. Your strategy will not work 100% of the time but if you can have one that works at least more than half the time then you are heading along the right track, also remembering to have a strict risk management strategy in place.

So here we are listing a few pointers on things you can do or use to have a solid strategy...

Keep everything *simple!* We have discovered this from all our years of learning about forex trading. We mentioned this earlier and doing so again because it will help especially in the early stages of your trading journey. Do not overdo things or over complicate them, because the fact is, it really does not need to be very complicated.

Examine *economic* data and global news every day, whether you are trading or not. Before you start your day, you could take a look at all the events in the financial calendar, read the newspaper or watch the news so you are aware of major events going on, upcoming and also if there is any volatility that may occur in the charts.

Embodying the likes of a lion, a soldier, a wolf or someone who is out to *hunt* and gain wealth in the industry of trading is essential. Sounds crazy, but for us, it is needed for the right mind set and helps in making a conscious decision to becoming an elite in forex trading. You may find that this information will prove to be beneficial in the long run and please this doesn't mean hate things or people or act in a way that is not positive but it means that you should be strict, confident, precise, and always alert with your trading.

Set yourself some pointers or a *checklist*, where all boxes have to be ticked off or activated before you place any given trade. This is where confluence and probability come into play; you can do more studying on this independently. For example, you may say to yourself that 'before I place any trade; I need to at least see the ABCD pattern forming, I need to see an engulfing candlestick formed assisting my prediction and it needs to match four different timeframes before I place a trade and if not all these boxes are ticked then don't trade'. Your checklist could consist of as many points as you wish, it's all down to your preferences.

SPECIAL BONUS SECTION

Welcome to the best part of the guidebook! You know what they say...save the best for last. We hope you have enjoyed the journey so far and have learnt a lot, so that you can take in this information and implement into your trading careers and your lives in general.

This section will give you direct sources, tips and knowledge on building a better trading style and acquiring wealth. It is deliberately made simple and easy-to-grasp as we want you all to benefit from all the great information out there, plus we just want you to do some extra studying! Enjoy!

THE MAJOR FX PAIRS & NICKNAMES

Trading pairs with high volatility has proved to be more profitable as the volumes are much higher. The forex pairs with high volatility are usually the major currency pairs, which we have listed below with their fancy nicknames. It is good to trade these pairs because there is more movement and opportunity for you to make profits whereas if there were hardly any movement in the market you cannot make as much money. This also depends on the type of person and trader you are, as you might prefer range bound trends because you can scalp. But here is the popular terminology…

GBP / USD	USD / CAD
EUR / JPY	NZD / USD
USD / JPY	EUR / USD
AUD / USD	USD / CHF
GBP / JPY	EUR / GBP

AUD/USD – Aussie
GBP/JPY – Guppy
GBP/USD – Cable
EUR/GBP – Chunnel
EUR/JPY – Yuppy
EUR/USD – Fiber

NZD/USD – Kiwi
USD/CAD – Beaver/Loonie
USD/CHF – Swissy
USD/JPY – Ninja

BROKERS TO PICK FROM

Choosing a broker might be one of the most difficult steps when starting your trading journey, so we have provided a selection below that we believe are good and you can pick from these if you wish. You can try a few different ones on a demo account and see which one best suits you and choose the one that you prefer. Take into consideration the features, tools, ease of use and credibility, you might want to do some research before you sign up. Good luck!

Oanda
FXCM
Plus 500
CMC Markets
ThinkForex
IG web platform
Spreadbet
Intertrader
ETX Capital
City Index

20 GREAT WEBSITES & SOURCES TO ASSIST YOU ON YOUR NEW JOURNEY

As a team at Money Luxury, we understand how hard it is to find a reliable and credible source to learn from and to understand more about the finance and investment industry. We had to go to space and back to narrow this down through years of studying. So we have decided to speed up this time for our readers by providing you with a comprehensive list of the best websites to learn from, utilise, socialise on, network with investors, traders, entrepreneurs and people similar to yourself who may have the same vision, interests and drive. They contain popular news sources, some exclusive forums, investor glossary and more! So have a look at them and enjoy!

AnnualReports.co.uk
Bloomberg.com
CityAM.com
CNBC.com
DailyFx.com
DailyTelegraph.co.uk/Finance
Forbes.com
ForexFactory.com
FXStreet.com
Investopedia.com
InvestorWords.com

MarketWatch.com
Money.com
MSN.com/Money
MyFXBook.com
ThinkForex.com
TradingView.com
Urbanforex.com
WSJ.com
Yahoo.com/finance

TOP 10 BOOKS ON TRADING & BUILDING WEALTH

Knowledge is power! This is why we have created a list of some of the best books for you to learn a great deal from and to expand your knowledge, not just about the forex market but about wealth and life in general. Even if you are one of those people who just never seem to finish reading a book from front to back, we're sure you would with some of the great choices listed below.
Getting into the habit of reading and learning is key to building wealth and getting closer to the goal of earning a million, so if being a book nerd is what it's going to take, then so be it!

10 Essentials of Forex trading by Jared F. Martinez
Naked Forex by Alex Nekritin and Walter Peters
The Forex Mindset by Jared F. Matinez
Extraordinary Delusions and Madness of Crowd by Charles Mackay
The Crowd by Gustave Le Bon
Think and Grow Rich by Napoleon Hill
Rich Dad Poor Dad by Robert Kiyosaki
Global Macro Trading by Greg Liner
Rich Dad's Guide to Investing by Robert Kiyosaki
The Alchemy of Finance by George Soros

13 GOLDEN TIPS FROM MONEY LUXURY

Now we have reached the finale of En Route To A Million, volume 1. This section is a bonus we decided to give to you guys free of charge; this information is priceless and very well thought out, which has been created through years of learning of the industry, which could possibly save you years of pain and time. Don't take everything in here as your gospel, but it has worked for us; so use what applies to your personality and style of living or trading.

1) Have a *reason* to achieve your goal that is *bigger than you*. Have an underlying aim that resonates with your heart, for example it could be to pay for your parents' mortgage, making sure they never have to work again, or starting a charity organisation for a cause you really have interest in or it could be to change the world…just find something.

2) *Training the mind to be positive* and *open* is crucial in trading and also in life. This gives you more opportunities to succeed and benefits from the time you invest because you will see things in a better light, which

is not only good for your mind but also for your sanity. The saying *'I never lose, I either win or I learn'* relates to being positive and open minded, something that we at Money Luxury live by.

3) *Focus* on *learning* from mistakes! Being skilled and educated on this point is priceless. If you can learn to train your mind and actions to *never* repeat the same mistakes then you are on your way to a great and successful road. Think about it!

4) *Saving money* at all costs is very important when you are trying to build wealth, as you will need extra finances for investment opportunities and even just for a rainy day. People who spend and do not save will eventually realise that they have no money left. *Spend less* than you earn is one of the pointers that many millionaires say was one of the things that helped them get to where they are. For example, if you have made £2 one day, then spend no more than £1.99 that day (should be less, but you get the drift).

5) *Make money from ideas* and various income streams to use partially for trading and vice versa; use trading profits for developing the ideas. This one is for the entrepreneurs and aspiring entrepreneurs: create a business or an idea that can generate some extra income and use part of this income to invest in your trading account. The reason for this is for a major topic in trading and a term that we spoke on earlier, which is *compounding*. To understand and to keep it simple; the more money you have in your trading account, the more

money you can make; so once you have learnt to accumulate pips and become a professional, you may decide to scale up your stake size and need not catch as much as you may have if you had a smaller account size. Get it?

6) It is always a good idea to *invest*; whether short term or long term, as this will enable you to make profit on a continuous basis. You remember the saying 'Do not put all your eggs in one basket', well this is another good time to use it, when it comes to investing you need to learn to diversify. Earning not only earned income but also passive income, though we will not go into that in this book *(maybe in our next volume)* but study and learn about the different ways to invest and build a portfolio.

7) *Never* be *greedy* and *always* be *grateful* for whatever you make, even if it is just £5 for the day. Even if you make a loss, just take it on the chin and analyse why you lost the money and learn from it. Learn to appreciate *every pound* and situation when trading. When you begin to trade more often, after a few wins it is easy to lose sight of the fact that every winning trade still is positive in the end. The market can be extremely ruthless with no care in the world about traders so even if it gives you £1, be happy and grateful.

8) *Learn the art* of closing; this is a quote that was noted when heard from a professional trader at a trading seminar in London. It did not resonate at first but once more experience was gained from trading it was clear what was said. This is key as you read earlier, that the

market is driven by fear and greed; which is the cause of why 95% of traders lose their money; they did not know when to close their trade.

9) Constantly *find new mentors* and investors if you strongly believe in yourself. This is important, as you will always need guidance and people that will invest in you and your business for it to reach the next level. So always soak in information, network and rub shoulders with people who are more experienced and have more knowledge as you may find it was just one bit of information or investing that was needed to take you to the next level.

10) Best way to learn is to *teach*, that is one of the reasons you are reading this right now. We understand that the more we teach, the better we also become at trading because we are going over and revising all the topics we have learnt and are passing on to you, so all in all, it is a win-win situation for both parties. So try and start teaching someone, obviously once you understand the industry yourself.

11) Dress how you want to be dressing if you were the manager at a well-established company that you really like. Maybe you might want to just dress like you are ready for your office job *daily*. We all know the saying 'Dress to impress', well that is basically it. When you dress well it gives you a sense of confidence and people take towards you more. This ultimately can make you a better trader as you will feel good about yourself and you may meet people that can benefit or help you along your

journey just because you wore a well fitted suit to an event.

12) *Strive* to be the *best*, be the best at everything you do, always be the hardest worker in the room and aim to leave a legacy behind. This is another powerful goal to set yourself and if followed religiously, it can take you to heights that you could not have dreamed of. One way to keep this in mind is to compete with yourself every day, so from now on you can always aim to be better than the person you were yesterday.

13) Finally *create* a *legacy* and build it slowly. This is a motivational pointer for the people who strive to be great and successful. It is an ambitious goal but you know what they say 'Aim for the stars and land on the moon', which means that you should always dream big.
Although leaving a legacy is a big dream, it is important to grasp the fact that it will not happen overnight, so take small little steps every day. This will give you something to work for every day, a reason to jump out of bed! Even when you just want to repeatedly press the snooze button on your alarm and have a lay in…

So… unfortunately this brings us to the end… until next time…we are going to miss you but will make sure we meet again sometime soon.

Stay tuned, stay en route!

Cheerio

Printed in Great Britain
by Amazon